DUBLIN, RAHENY
and me

JUNE COOKE

DEDICATION

To Liam – friend, husband, father and
grandfather par excellence .

CONTENTS

POEMS

Where do they come from, all those words,

that push themselves into my captive mind,

demanding to be liberated, given voice,

committed to virgin page, blank, unread,

using me as a tool this world to find?

Thoughts expressed may seem like mine alone,

pale descriptions from my wondering sight,

opinions on issues serious or banal,

emotions flowing fast from obscure depths,

relying on me to give them a life and light.

Where do they come from, all those words,

claiming their right to be released by me,

guiding my pen to make their message heard,

using the music of verse to make it plain?

A puzzled poet, I must write to set them free.

RAHENY I

Written for the unveiling of the Raheny Millenium Clock, 2002.

Smugglers operated centuries ago from the sandy seashore near.

A country village round the Rath of Eanna's small stone church was here.

Time passed and history changed the face of the local lands,

The imported gentry took over this sear area near the sands.

One local estate was huge and owned by a family of brewing fame,

Others were large and powerful too and bore many a famous name,

Nineteenth century progress brought the mighty railway through,

The great Liberator Daniel O'Connell came and spoke and his words came true,

Twentieth century freedom saw a phenomenal growth,

Our little village prospered and grew between Dublin City and Howth.

One thousand years of Baile Atha Cliath celebrated in '88,

Raheny began it and all through that year the village people were great.

A new millennium dawned and history's tale continues on,

The village of Raheny and it's people have not gone,

With churches, schools, shops and houses and now a beautiful clock,

A friendly, hardworking community, it cannot come as a shock,

That the future looks bright for this village near the city and the sea,

Ancient and modern Raheny is a wonderful place to be.

ME

I tried to grow pink roses,

And tulips tall and red,

Nasturtium seeds I planted,

But weeds grew up instead.

I baked sweet apple tarts,

Forgot the sugar, they were foul,

My chocolate sponge was hard and flat,

I didn't cry, I howled.

Then I tried to paint the kitchen

Yellow, clean and bright,

Dropped the paintpot on the floor,

The cleanup took all night.

Dressmaking attracted me,

Bought material and thread,

Couldn't do sleeves or straighten hems,

In shame I hung my head.

I put a plaster on Timmy's knee,

And kissed away the pain of his fall,

His "I love you Mammy" mended my heart,

I'm not hopeless after all.

FIRST PRIMROSE OF SPRING

S – MALL GREEN LEAVES, SWEET SCENTED PETALS,

P – ALE, BUT AT THE HEART, A GOLDEN RING,

R – ISEN, DEFIANT, THROUGH FROST HARD EARTH, BUT

I – N MY HAND, SUCH A FRAGILE THING,

N – OW, BLEAK WINTER HAS BEEN VANQUISHED,

G – LORIOUS PRIMROSE, NOW, IS SPRING.

LOVE

Our eyes met, yours smiled I thought,

We slowly walked towards each other,

I noticed your tie, and your wavy hair,

That was the start of our love.

I walked up the aisle all dressed in white,

You turned and I laid my hand in yours,

Two gold rings and a marriage was made,

A testimony of our love.

Two little girls and then two boys,

With pride we watched them develop and grow,

Nursing, guiding, these precious flowers,

The product of our love.

Thinning hair and sagging muscles,

Portly figures which once were trim,

Greeting old age as a rest from our labours,

Thankful of our love.

Our life story is nearly over,

We shared hopes and sorrows and joys.

And our greatest joy, oh! Wonderful joy,

Was the sharing of our love.

THE MAN AROUND THE CORNER

The man around the corner, you know the one I mean,

He wears a beard and a black knitted hat and he is often to be seen

Walking around Raheny, he always has a grin and a wave,

For everyone he meets, he is from St. Anne's, and his name is Dave.

It's a beautiful day, he'll call to you as you run for the bus to town

And you have to smile at his cheerfulness when the rain is pouring down.

Listen to the whispering trees, he will say, they love the April showers,

And as soon as the Earth soaks up the water, we will get beautiful flowers.

He will use the cupla focail, if he thinks you are of that kind,

He is a gentleman, is Dave and he has a cultured mind.

The world around him gives him joy in pouring rain for bright sunshine,

I am glad the man around the corner is a friend of mine.

LIVING IN SAINT ANNE'S

First came hundreds of houses,

Standing row by row,

When people arrived to spend their lives,

A community started to grow.

Hardworking men with hardworking wives,

Raising many a daughter and son,

Who studied and worked and prospered,

Bringing pride to everyone.

Through the years some passed on,

Some decided to move away,

But most of us who came to St. Anne's,

Have been delighted to stay.

Times have changed and so have we,

Nothing remains the same,

Life in St. Anne's is different,

But most are still glad they came.

What the future holds no one can say,

Though we all have hopes and plans,

But I predict it will always be,

Really good living in St. Anne's.

GUIDES

To commemorate the 60th anniversary of the founding of the organisation.

Who was she, the first girl guide,

Who wore the uniform,

Did she have a sense of destiny,

With pride was her heart warm.

Did she visualise the thousands,

Who would follow where she strode,

Along the path of guiding,

A bright, exciting road.

I joined the Brigini,

Young and small and scared,

I was introduced to the maxim,

Bi ullamh, be prepared.

I studied the Aspirant test,

The prayer and promise too,

The day of my enrolment,

Was like all my dreams come true.

Then as a guide I worked to earn,

Those precious leader's stripes,

Doing merit badges and polishing brass,

Until my mother ran out of wipes.

And all the time I was making friends,

Sharing my laughter and tears,

Finding companions who took my hand,

And have walked with me all through the years.

Captain Eithne Morris set standards so high,

For Buion Bainrioghan na hEireann to reach,

District Captain Eileen McCormack,

Spurred us on to the Shield, with her speech.

Commissioner Macklin, she was equal to God,

Inspected us, oh! How we sweated,

Would everyone's tunic be perfectly pressed,

Would we know the Guide Law, or forget it,

Would our sheep shank shortening pass the test,

Did our buckles shine like gold,

Were our berets on straight and our shoelaces tied,

And our reef knots a joy to behold.

Well we won the Shield, and not only once,

But Guiding wasn't all work,

I made my stage debut on the rally,

With a tea towel on my head, I was a Turk.

My first campfire was a wonderful thing,

I had always enjoyed making rhymes,

Soon my songs entered the repertoire,

And we sang these many times.

One lady I learned to respect and then love,

The Commissioner known as O'D,

Riding on her donkey,

She is unforgettable to me.

Then there were hikes, and there were camps,

Then a company of my own,

A new generation of eager girls,

This great guiding life to be shown.

I'm just an Associate member now,

My old uniform's up in the attic,

But, once a guide always a guide,

And I don't care if that sounds dramatic.

I was taught about loyalty, honour and trust,

Lifeskills and hobbies besides,

When someone remarks on a job I can do now,

I say, I learnt that in the guides.

Yes that first girl guide sixty years ago,

Was the start of a marvelous movement,

The uniform has changed,

But the guiding ethic has never needed improvement,

Girls growing into womanhood,

Sharing faith and duty and joy,

And friendship, the very essence of guiding,

That time can never destroy.

PEACEFUL HOUSECATS

Elephants really don't like mice,

Mice make them trumpet and roar and run,

Yet peaceful housecats hunt mice and then

Throw them up in the air for fun.

Little boys really hate to wash,

Bathrooms are a nightmare to any boy.

Yet peaceful housecats wash every inch of fur,

Purring as they do it in obvious joy.

Dogs chase balls and cars and cats,

Barking excitedly, brave and fearless,

Yet peaceful housecats hiss and scratch,

And dogs turn tail and run off cheerless.

Some people like to keep cats as pets,

Feeding, grooming and mourning their loss,

When peaceful housecats leave home without warning,

Not lost, just showing their people who is boss.

Man has conquered the world with his knowledge and science,

Labouring hard until he can barely crawl,

Yet peaceful housecats just living for pleasure,

Are petted and pampered and loved by all.

There is no justice in the world.

MY SWEET VALENTINE

I dreamed of a valentine handsome and rich,

Saying I love you, I love you, I love you,

A lawyer, a banker, I didn't care which,

As long as he whispered I love you.

I pictured him bringing me chocolates and flowers,

Taking me to a ball and dancing for hours,

Whis-per-ing gently That tune, it is ours,

For I love you, I love you, I love you.

My lover and I, we would walk to the park,

Saying I love you, I love you, I love you.

He'd go down on one knee right there in the dark,

Saying I love you, I love you, I love you.

He'd give me a diamond ring, sparkly and bright,

Id answer Yes and we'd kiss in the night,

And plan a great future just filled with delight,

Saying I love you, I love you, I love you.

Then I heard Johnny who hasn't a penny,

Saying I love you, I love you, I love you.

He's small with crossed eyes and hair hasn't any,

But he whispers I love you, I love you.

He gives me a crossbar cos he hasn't a car,

We share bags of chips and a pint in the bar,

He's no genius, I know and he'll never go far,

But I tell him I love you, I love you.

I'll marry in August, the love of my life,

Saying I love you, I love you, I love you.

And I'll tell him each day when I am his wife,

I love you, I love you, I love you.

He'll never be handsome or wealthy, I know,

But my sweet valentine will be faithful and so,

We'll whisper each night time as older we grow,

I love you, I love you, I love you.

MOTHER OF THE BRIDE

We were invited to their home last week,

The parents-in-law to be,

He was suave and sophisticated,

A fashion plate was she.

Even their dog was thoroughbred,

A Cavalier King Charles,

Not a mongrel like our Rover,

Who drools and scratches and snarls.

Next week they're coming to our house,

We're painting the garden shed,

And I'm practicing making soufflé,

Throwing out the houseplants that are dead.

I've threatened Granny she must wear her teeth,

And not tell ours guests of her bunions,

Bobby's been warned to eat all his dinner,

Even the sauce and the onions.

The only people not bothered,

Are the groom to be, and the bride,

They stand holding hands as we fluster and fuss,

Their joy too intense to hide.

I'll be glad when the wedding is over,

I'll probably laugh that I wept,

Forgotten will be the worry and work,

All these nights when I haven't slept.

Will my dieting work and my dress fit me right,

Or shall everyone think I look fat,

Should I change my hair colour, maybe go a bit blonde,

Do I look silly wearing a hat?

On my beautiful daughter's wedding,

I will put all these problems aside,

Smile and look happy playing my part,

As mother of the bride.

DUBLIN 1991

Europe, Europe, what is it? Where?

A vast and faceless continent, somewhere over there,

And I, blood run, tear soaked, young and ancient too,

Am Cultural Capital of Europe, and I am who?

I am Dublin, Baile an Atha Cliath,

Ireland's centre, the heart, An Lar,

Where walks the ghosts of dreamers, schemers,

And believers in Eire go Brath.

James Joyce made my people, The Dubliners, famed,

And The Dubliners, chorused my songs,

Brendan Behan, The Hostage of his own troubled soul,

Chronicled terrible wrongs.

Myles na Gopaleen, or Flann O'Brien,

Laughed, and showed everyone how,

And the humour, the wit, still drips from the pen,

Hugh Leonard is holding it now.

Here, out of tragedy, beauty was born,

Christy Brown brought us Down all the Days,

Struggling to prove the giant he was,

And succeeding, in so many ways.

Some made us laugh, with their silvery tongues,

Cecil Sheridan, Jack Cruise, Jimmie O'Dea,

Maureen Potter, Des Keogh and many more,

Are still giving us comedy.

The wonderful music of Sean O'Riada, honour to me brings,

John O'Connor plays his piano, and Bernadette Greevy sings,

Bob Geldoff, with music, fed millions who hungered,

The echo of Live aid, still clings.

Painters too, like Jack B. Yeats, gave my beauty fame.

Actors in theatre, and on film, glorify my name.

The whole world has tasted my dark, creamy, brew.

And agrees that Guinness is good for you.

All tremble with fear of Bram Stoker's Dracula,

Swift's Gulliver's Travels thrilled many,

Joyce's Ulysses still puzzles the scholars,

They search for meaning, if any.

Oscar Fingall O'Flaherty Wilde,

Made the Ballad of Reading Gaol,

Yeats, O'Casey, Shaw and Synge,

Made all other literature seem pale.

When Beckett was Waiting for Godot, forever,

The world watched, with bated breath,

Yes, my people tell stories, which hold all enthralled,

Of love and of life and of death.

And my children's names will be written,

In letters of shining gold,

When the story of this World's history,

Of cultural endeavour is told.

So, Cultural Capital of Europe I am,

I bear the title with pride,

Through my people, their art, their writing and deeds,

Dublin City is known, far and wide.

SPRINGTIME IN ST ANNE'S

A squirrel, half seen flash of bushy tail and russet coat,

Disappearing up a new dressed tree,

And through the canopy of fresh green leaves,

A tantalizing glimpse of azure sea.

Along the winding mossgrown path a glossy blackbird toils,

Doing his best to lift a twig, too long,

Intent upon the task of building nest,

With mate to please he has no time for song.

Over in the shady corner where the grass is left uncut,

A deep sweet lake of bluebells spreads,

And scattered all around, the daffodils,

Dance to the breeze, tossing golden heads.

Trilling joyously on living thrusting branch and timeworn rock,

Feathered songsters tunefully fill the air,

A softly buzzing bumblebee goes after his work,

And look, I see a rabbit over there.

Just hatched duckling tentatively swimming on the pond,

Everywhere new life, by nature's plans,

Privileged, I stand, and watching, marvel,

At the glory of Springtime in Saint Anne's.

NATURE KNOWS

When you passed no fanfares sounded,

No more than had lauded your every day,

Bustling humanity, busy, unknowing,

Shared your journey but did not see,

Scarcely a ripple on life's pond,

Marked your coming and going again,

No scientific discoveries made,

Theatre handbills don't boast of your fame,

On library lists your name is not mentioned,

Genes unpassed, your children unborn.

Once you bandaged a jackdaws wing,

You told the story in the pub,

The fish you caught in the river was big,

But you put him back in the water again,

Once you planted daffodil bulbs,

Year after year they bloom in spring,

You praised the beauty of sea and land,

Tossing trees and myriad stars,

Little difference you made to the world,

But you lived, and nature knows.

INTO MANHOOD

The Captain urged on his loyal crew,

Heave ye ho, me hearties,

Forget your easy life ashore,

The dancing and the parties,

Girls that charmed you with smiling eyes,

Songs you sang at the bar,

Forget the land, with all it's ties,

Remember you're a tar.

Think only of the purse of money,

That every man of you knows,

I'll give to the lucky one who yells,

Skipper, there she blows.

Wind blew fiercely, waves towered high,

But the sailors' eyes were keen,

For six long days they scanned the sea,

No trace of a whale was seen,

On the seventh day, the galley lad,

A tow headed youth, but pale,

On his first trip abroad, with no sea legs yet,

He was leaning over the rail,

Hardly could he believe his eyes,

As a jet of water rose,

It was not far off, a whale! he yelled,

Skipper, there she blows.

All hands to the boats, a sighting, men,

To starboard, three lengths distant,

The Captain gave orders, all boats, more speed,

Crewmen obeyed on the instant,

Fire the harpoons before he dives,

You've got him, good work, now hold,

The battle raged on, 'twas a might beast,

Fast, and cunning, and bold,

They won at last and hauled it astern,

The galley lad blushed to his toes,

When Captain and crew raised three cheers for his yell,

Skipper there she blows.

THE STORM

March many weathers, the sages say,

Comes in like a lion, goes out like a lamb,

And the tides, the tides are high,

And wild and fierce and unpredictable.

Lorna and Seamus looked down from the hill,

Where, hand in hand, they stood,

The air was sharp, but the sea lay calm,

The weather forecast was good,

They saw, below in the harbour,

Lorna's father, and brothers Tom and Fred,

Dwarfed by distance but easily known,

For each had a golden head.

Their trawler, Orion, lay anchored but ready,

Awaiting the turn of the tide,

When the fleet would set out for the herring beds,

Where the sea was deep and wide.

Six trawlers, six crews and six laden nets,

Would return with a silvery treasure,

To celebrate Easter, and the wedding,

Of Lorna and Seamus, who, lost in the pleasure,

Of their love and their dreams,

Forgot to watch them go,

Ignored the chill, didn't notice the dark,

Or the wind that began to blow.

But arms entwined and lips atingle,

With mutual delight,

They planned a rosy future,

Until far into the night.

Then strolling back down by the harbour wall,

They saw the waves were white capped and tall,

Racing clouds had the moon obscured,

But to stiff coastal breeze they were inured,

And wrapped as they were in the aura of love,

They felt secure and bless'd,

And paid no heed to the warning signs,

Of the oncoming tempest.

Out at sea, Tom and Fred and their Father,

Struggled to pull in the nets,

Pounding waves crashed over the side of the boat,

And they were cold and wet.

In the distance the lights of the other trawlers,

Bobbing up and down,

Seemed too far away,

Fred consulted the compass with a worried frown.

They were miles off course, drifting, helpless,

Tossed by wind and wave,

Feverishly fumbling they sent up distress flares,

But who would see, who'd come to save?

The Orion overturned!

Only lifejackets now, between them and a watery grave.

In the wispy light of a stormy dawn,

Five trawlers limped to shore,

The alarm was raised, but all feared,

The Orion and her crew were no more.

Ring the bell, ring the bell for the lifeboat,

Men came running fast,

Seamus jumped aboard pulling on his sou'wester,

Just as the line was cast.

For a long miserable day,

Lashed by torrential rain,

Wives, lovers, sons and mothers,

And Lorna, waited in vain,

Till as night fell, a shout,

Look, out there, a light,

The lifeboat was returning,

Lorna shivered with fright.

Oh, my God, let them be safe,

My father and my brothers,

And please, let Seamus be safe in the lifeboat,

And every one of the others.

Slowly, so agonizingly slowly,

The craft drew near, and then,

Anxious eyes strained to count the number on board,

To recognise the men.

A shaft of moonlight glinted on three gold heads,

Lorna trembled in bliss,

Thank you, God, and oh! there's Seamus,

Lorna blew him a kiss.

So, joy bells rang out that Easter day,

The sun shone bright and warm,

Prayers of thanksgiving were offered up,

For the men newly saved from the storm.

Rice and confetti filled the air,

People laughed, and two mothers cried,

As Seamus, the hero, pledged his life and love,

To Lorna, his golden haired bride.

SURVIVAL

The March air, crisp and clear, carried the sound for many miles,

Across barren empty fields, along narrow, winding roads,

To the little cottage homesteads and the big house on the hill.

A clarion calling the people to pray, and they came,

In answer to the bell, carrying the seed, the precious seed,

Their only chance for future food, their only hope for life.

Molly Murphy, pale thin quiet, slowly followed her father and mother,

Greeting neighbours with subdued voice,

Kinsfolk and friends, with one purpose, one dream.

SURVIVAL.

On the feast of Patrick, in the small cold chapel,

They laid their treasure at the altar,

On each tuber every eye carefully noted for therein lay their salvation,

Peter O'Flynn, last of his clan, lowered his burden and took his place,

And where parents, siblings and two maiden aunts had prayed,

There was empty space, as space there was in row and row,

For many had perished at terrible '45 and still more dreadful '46,

When blight had laid waste to their crop,

Now after black '47 they gathered to pray, storming Heaven for

SURVIVAL.

Beneath the sod in the barren yard outside,

Lay those whose dreams had withered away,

The weak went first, but empty bellies,

Fell even the strongest, fiercest, stout,

And those years were a long time to hunger.

Father Byrne lifted his arms, Hear us, Lord, we beg,

Heed not our sins but let this seed grow clean,

Send drying wind and warming sun, and gentle, greening rain,

Rescue your people, feed us Lord, we implore you for

SURVIVAL.

They went to the fields and planted the seed,

And the breeze blew sweetly gentle, for days and weeks of waiting,

And watching and hoping and much despair,

Blossom came, creamy, beautiful, promising, but did it hide the
dreaded rot?

On the haulms, faint yellowing lightened the green,

And anxious nostrils quested for the telltale, sickly smell,

Peter O'Brien, now the youngest householder was first to make the cut,

The fork went deep, and with a mighty heave he turned the soil,

Exposing, potatoes, not plentiful, but healthy,

SURVIVAL.

Word spread fast over hill and dale, to cottage, manse and chapel,

We're saved, we're saved, the crop is good,

At last we have outlived the famine.

Molly told Peter she would be Mrs. O'Flynn, people danced and sang,

Songs not heard since before the disaster,

Of life and love, and bountiful land, and the future,

The wonderful future at hand, with starvation a thing of the past,

Father Byrne raised a mighty alleluia, his flock made echo, louder,

And each upstretched hand held God's marvelous gift, perfect potatoes,

SURVIVAL.

FEDERATION OF WOMEN'S CLUBS 50TH

Congratulations Ladies, well done.

We have laughed together and sometimes cried,

Found our horizons widen,

Discovered talents we never knew we had,

And projects we could take pride in.

Singing, dancing, acting, writing,

Arts and crafts and debating too,

Public speaking, travel, nights out, ten pin bowling,

We made friends and had so much to do,

Others less fortunate than ourselves,

We helped in a myriad of ways,

Gaining team spirit and leadership skills,

That will benefit us all of our days.

Homes in Africa, neo natal cots in Dublin,

Clothing, vests, hats, scarves, and gloves galore,

Cancer services and hospices we helped,

And other charities, many more.

Let us join our hands together now,

On this happy day of celebration,

Rejoice, for fifty golden years of our Federation.

CHRIS

Chris was my friend, more than my friend,

A lifelong fellow guide,

We worked, played and laughed together,

She held my hand when I cried.

Past members on a Thursday night,

Headquarters echoed with laugher,

We all shared each other's sorrows and joys,

Then raced for the last bus after.

Fernhill really made our summers great,

Children's dinner, the fancy dress,

At the silver strand we paid at the gate,

On duty Chris was the best.

Eddie made us laugh at weekends,

They're together once more, that's our loss,

She won't be starting the sing song again,

As our president, Chris was the boss.

Chris loved her children and reared them well,

She was gentle, but her voice was loud,

No meant no, but her hugs were sweet,

And it worked, they have done her proud.

Anne, and Cathy, and Janet,

John and Paul and Denise,

You had a wonderful mother,

Take comfort, for she is at peace.

NEWGRANGE

Many walked here before us, and wondered,

At the mystery of this place,

Silent stones ever watching, waiting

Hiding triumph or disgrace.

Some say kings were buried here,

Warriors, heroes all,

Their deeds of valor long ago,

Lost beyond recall.

Learned people who studied the sky,

Knew the heavens well,

The passage of the sun they could,

With accuracy tell.

Setting stone on stone to build,

A circle mounded tall,

With giant standing boulders round,

Set deeply, not to fall.

At the winter solstice only,

Narrow passage led,

To chamber sunlit bright as day,

Wherein lay the dead.

None can say for certain now,

If druids chanted here,

Or felons or sacrificial maids,

Trembled in mortal fear.

Did these stones run red with blood,

Or echo terrified cry,

The captured sunlight then disclose,

Victims bound to die.

This grass we tread was trampled on,

By our fathers now long dead,

They knew the secrets hidden here,

Understood, but never said.

Kings or peasants, champions or foes,

Nameless in death and time,

Faces forgotten, histories untold,

In drama, tale or mime.

So stand we now at this awful place,

Feeling the ancient fear,

Sensing the presence of long gone men,

Wondering what happened here.

SEARCH

There is a hunger here that cannot be assuaged,

By beer, or cars, or cigarettes,

Or wealth, or Ecstasy.

There is a crying voice that cannot be stilled,

By travel, or music, or copulation,

Or art, or pornography.

There is a need that cannot be satisfied,

By belief, or penance, or devotion.

Or Mass, or rosary.

There is an answer that cannot be undiscovered,

By us, or crime, or worldwide wars,

Or rape, or cruelty.

Will prevail, and we will be lost.

TO MY NANNY IN PORTMARNOCK

I loved your little wooden house,

Pink roses scrambling all around the door,

Drinking water in a bucket in the corner,

Blue lino mat with three fat penguins on the floor.

Spiders always live in wooden houses,

Ours were big, brown, furry, round and fat

With long legs and eyes so evil looking,

They even scared our brave old tabby cat.

Candlelight made shadows on the walls,

Weird shapes that filled my heart with dread,

My squeaky childish voice joined yours in prayer,

When each night we said the rosary in bed.

I loved our morning treks across the fields,

Collecting mushrooms for a breakfast treat,

Picking blackberries in the lane, making jam

With apples from our tree, too sour to eat.

You taught me how to crochet and to sew,

Make daisy chains and sandcastles to swim,

Tales of ancient Ireland, some myth, some very true,

Like cruel Cromwell, folk were all afraid of him.

You told of sun and stars and outer space,

How rockets would go up and make new finds,

You always seemed so clever and so wise

And yet you fed the goldfish rasher rinds.

I loved our evening walks along the strand,

Moonshine laid sparkling diamonds on the brine,

The panorama of sea and sky and sand,

Just two sets of footprints, yours and mine.

Now the little house we shared is gone,

The little girl you taught and loved is grown

But all the wonderful memories linger on,

Of magical summers you and I have known.

MAKING TRACKS

Celebrating the 150th Anniversary of the opening of the Dublin and Drogheda Rail

The spring of eighteen hundred and thirty five,

Was cold and very wet,

In the Drogheda shebeen a farmer grumbled,

His weather worn face hard set.

Tom Brodigan sat in his old grey frieze coat,

Listening, agreeing, and thinking,

Seeking a solution to their transport problems,

As the two exhausted friends sat drinking.

Just back from Dublin, a business trip,

Over a hard bumpy road, for six long hours,

At five shillings on the Mail Coach, an outside seat,

Lashed by sharp wind and heavy showers.

Brodigan had seen in the city,

Trains that ran to Kingstown and back,

And suddenly he knew the answer,

What they needed was a railway track.

Tom put a notice in the newspapers,

Calling for backers and support,

Said a rail link between Dublin and Drogheda,

Would bring benefits of every sort.

Lord Talbot, Lord Howth and twenty five others,

Met on a fine August day,

Formed a company for the project,

The Grand Northern Trunk Railway.

Then the trouble started,

Two different routes were proposed,

One running inland through Navan to Armagh,

The other along the coast,

To keep the trains from Marino,

Lord Charlemont voted inland,

Engineer William Cubbitt favoured,

The coastal route near the strand.

The sea-siders won in thirty six,

When Royal Assent was gained,

Compulsory purchase of lands for the tracks,

Made many friendships strained.

Four hundred men under William Weekes,

Dug and shoveled and shifted great stones,

One poor labourer, Owen Kenny, run over by a cart,

Lost a leg and broke many bones.

Long was the toil and many the hitches,

Till the great day in forty four,

When the tracks were ready for the mighty trains,

To travel as never before.

Daniel O'Connell, the Liberator,

Rode a train to Raheny's fast built station,

And was feted and toasted at Edenmore House,

On the eve of the inaugural celebration.

Norah Creinah was the first engine,

The start of an honourable list,

For a hundred and fifty years they've run,

And scarcely a day they've missed.

In nineteen forty seven the Enterprise,

Could go non-stop Dublin to Belfast,

And by nineteen sixty all steam engines,

Were replaced by diesel at last.

Then came Dublin Area Rapid Transit,

The bright green beautiful DART,

If Tom Brodigan saw his railway now,

He'd have a song in his heart.

And that's not the end for the Arrow has come,

Improving our travel again,

Running on to the twenty first century,

A clean, fast and comfortable train.

TED CORCORAN
World International President of Toastmasters

In the far off kingdom of Kerry some few years ago,

A young lad looked over a railway bridge and dreamed,

He dreamed of adventure, travel, fame and fortune too,

The trains were his path to the future so it seemed.

Lights from Dublin beckoned, the kingdom he left behind,

Wooed and wed Celine, and Baldoyle became home,

Two sweet daughters gladdened Ted Corcoran's life,

He still watched trains and dreamed but didn't roam.

A friend said, try toastmasters, clubs for old and young,

Places to grow and learn your views to air,

Ted was keenly interested, for he had a silver tongue,

In the Hollybrook that night he took the chair.

Ted established Fingal Club, he started five in fact,

And gathered honours as he went along his way,

From C.T.M. up, step by step, courage he never lacked,

Until he got to the top, the place he stands today.

Teaching, entertaining, making friends galore,

Always ready to tell a tale or just advise,

Leading District 71, Fingal Club and more,

Liked for his wit and respected because he was wise.

Praise, objectives, suggestions, and encouragement too,

The lad from the kingdom gladly imparted to all,

Now president, toastmasters international is true,

Irishman Ted Corcoran is the pride of Fingal.

UPLIFT

There we stood, in this skyscraper lift,

This posh, mink coated lady, and me,

And a farmer's wife, obviously up for the day,

They were both very well off, I could see,

And I felt so shabby in my old cloth coat,

And my down at heel shoes, beside them,

But, ah! It's hard to keep smart, with only the dole,

For myself and six kids, and my Jem,

God love him, he's the salt of the earth.

Anyway, we were nearing the top, when the lift got struck,

Halfway between two floors,

Let me out! Let me out! yelled the culchie,

And she battering at the doors.

I have to catch a train at Heuston at six,

To go home and milk forty cows,

And lock up my chickens safe for the night,

And take care of my farrowing sows.

And Himself will come in from the fields for his dinner,

And not a scrap on the table,

He'll go and get drunk in the pub at the crossroads,

And end up asleep in the stable.

Don't be fretting, Mam, says I, sure your family'll help you,

Oh! No! she replied, between sobs,

Haven't they all come up to Dublin, and got Civil Service jobs,

Isn't that why I'm in the city now, to see if they're okay,

For they never visit, or write, at all, not since they went away.

But I've searched, and I couldn't find the place where they live,

My lovely daughters, and sons,

Yerra, what good's the new tractor, and the E.E.C. cheque,

When I've lost all my little ones.

Do pull yourself together, woman, said the fur-coated toff,

We all have our troubles, you know,

Even I, my husband has a mistress,

My son's in a weird religious sect,

But I don't let my heartache show.

Though my, once beautiful daughter, has bright green hair,

And gives herself cocaine shots,

And spends hours in our heated conservatory,

Growing marijuana in pots.

And our cook, she can't, and our gardener, he won't,

Now there's trouble in our villa in Spain,

Apparently the roof sprung a leak, last Thursday,

After some very un Spanishlike rain.

Well I listened to the pair of them and I said to myself,

Said I, sure money is not worth all that,

I'm better off with my Jem and his dole,

And our kids and our corporation flat.

Suddenly, we heard a voice from outside,

Hang on ladies, we'll soon have you free,

It was only a bit of a power cut,

It was the man from E.S.B.

At last, we stepped out of that horrible lift,

My two new found friends, and I,

I had no fur coat, no farm, I was shabby and poor,

But I held my head up high,

For I had riches beyond all price.

Six smashing kids and my darling Jem,

They had only money,

And I felt no envy as I stood in the street,

And waved goodbye to them.

MILLENIUM

Isn't it great gas, this Millennium thing, in 1988,

Dublin is 1000 years old, the city is en fete,

Imagine, we've been here for 1000 years, you know, one thing puzzles me,

Wouldn't you think after all that time flowing, the Liffey would have emptied into the sea.

Ah! You know you're in Dublin, when the buses are on strike,

And you can't afford a taxi, and someone's nicked your bike,

And you're set on, by a mugger, and knocked down to the ground,

You think your elbow's broken, but not a hospital can be found.

And even if there was one, they wouldn't treat you,

Because you haven't got ten pound.

And if you try to do some shopping, I'm telling you,

The prices! The prices are so bad,

Your money gets airsick, it flys so fast,

And your pocket only thinks your hands gone mad.

And Carmencita goes round smiling, saying Dublin's great, doing fine.

She doesn't have to manage, on the dole, no she's far from the breadline.

Still, look on the bright side, haven't we Sean Kelly, and Stephen Roche,

Irishman, Citizen Jack, and his soccer team, beyond reproach.

I wonder in another 1000 years, will there be still a Dublin town,

Or will all the people have emigrated and the buildings be all knocked down,

Will Carmencita Hederman be a well known historical name,

Will our Liffey still smell, our people still be great, and our problems just the same.

RAHENY II

To celebrate Raheny winning 'Best Village' Dublin Tidy Towns competition 2005.

Foxfield, Saint Assam's, Maywood, Saint Anne's,

Bettyglen, Lough Derg, Cill Eanna,

Where would you find these wonderful sites,

In Dublin's best village, Raheny.

Close by the city, near to the sea,

Served by the dart and the buses,

And as a bonus, we have the park,

Beautiful, lovely Saint Anne's.

That's where the squirrels and rabbits run free,

And walkers and sports people frolic,

Pitch and putt, hurling and football and tennis,

And model car racing as well.

We in Raheny breathe fresh clean air,

Thousands of trees do surround us,

Raheny is great, but best thing of all,

Our people are always so friendly.

We have a motto, Raheny be proud,

Let our community flourish,

All join together, sing it aloud,

Our village home is the best.

MY LIFE IN RAHENY

It was cold, so very cold, and dark and drear,

Sleet laden wind stung my face,

I shuddered, and tried to shield my infant sons,

March 29th, and of Spring, no trace.

Into the strange, unhomely house,

My tears mingled with theirs,

As I awaited the furniture van,

Bringing beds and tables and chairs.

It's miles from the city, so isolated,

Not even one shop nearby,

Town living family and friends had advised me,

Their logic I couldn't deny.

Just out of my teens, with a husband and two babies,

And a mortgage to last thirty years,

While outwardly scorning their forecasts of doom,

Inside I was a quivering mass of fears.

A knock on the door, a smiling woman,

With trayload of buns and tea,

Just to say welcome, and I hope you'll be happy,

And if you need anything, call on me.

My leaden heart took wings at her gesture, I smiled,

I had a neighbour, a friend, so soon,

She told me her name, and which house she lived in,

I said, My name is Cooke, call me June.

And so it began, my new life in Raheny,

A suburban village, in 1962,

My friends had been wrong, it was not isolated or lonely,

Though the shortage of shops was true.

Unknown faces mouthed Good morning, happy Easter,

After Mass in the old church, dark, cramped, so tiny,

I saw the new church, soon to be opened across the road,

It looked huge, all modern and shiny.

On my bicycle I explored the area around,

Saint Anne's Park was a joy to me,

The thatched cottage in Fox's lane, enchanting,

As was the view of Howth, across the shimmering sea.

BABYSITTING AISLING

Take care of the baby, of course I would,

The little pet, she is as good as gold,

I forgot I am not as young as I used to be,

Well, are not grannies supposed to be old.

The first shock I got was the luggage that came,

Buggy, walking pen, folding up cot,

A gigantic box of disposable nappies,

And a bright orange plastic pot.

A sterilizer for bottles and teats,

Tablets to dissolve in the water,

And carefully measured powdered milk,

To be fed to my little granddaughter.

A changing mat is a must, they said,

She is not used to being changed on the lap,

I knelt on the floor as she wriggled and squirmed,

And prayed that my back would not snap.

Her one-piece stretch garment had poppers to fasten,

Which to which I just did not know,

My children wore rompers and flannel nighties,

I am not used to a babygrow.

One thing has not changed, after powering,

Pampering, feeding and burping her well,

I sat on a chair and cuddled her closely,

She was ready for sleep, I could tell.

Quietly, I hummed an old nursery tune,

Wide eyed, she gazed, and then smiled,

Silken lashes drooped over petal soft cheeks,

My tears fell gently on my darling grandchild.

MY FRIEND IS A ROBIN

He comes to see me on a sunny day,

Hopping around my feet as if to say,

Have you any crumbs that you can spare,

Or do I have to go and beg elsewhere.

As I sit soaking up the sun I mentally plan,

For flowers I will plant next year if I can.

He never interrupts or interferes,

Robins do not plan ahead in years.

Living for the day, freedom to fly in the air,

And feast on what I throw him from my chair.

With a cheerful chirp my robin flies away,

Until hunger brings him back another day.

HAPPY MILLENIUM DUBLIN

Requested in honour of Dublin's Millennium for the Raheny-Dublin Millennium Presentation. Now in time capsule on O'Connell Street.

Dubhgalls and Fionngalls, the Vikings came,

The Irish named them Ostmen,

Near the Liffey's mouth lay a deep dark pool,

Their longboats could safely berth in.

Walls of mud and wattle rose,

Trade by barter flourished,

Pure fresh water and sweet green grass,

Kept swine and oxen nourished.

Native and foreigner mingled and bred,

Feasted and fought and buried their dead,

Built and rebuilt, layer on layer,

Till a fine new city was standing there,

Round the pool they called Dubh Linn.

I am Dublin, An Baila Atha Cliath,

City of a thousand years,

Thronged with a million citizens,

With their dreams, laughter and tears,

Echoed with plague, battle and famine,

Poverty, riches and glory,

Robbed my lifeblood by emigration,

Famed in song and story.

Rome has basilicas, Moscow has domes,

New Yorkers cluster in skyscraper homes,

Big Ben denotes London, an old leaning steeple makes Pisa,

But I have my people,

The wonderful people of Dublin.

Many times for faith and freedom,

Since Sitric and Brian Boru bled,

Heroes have fallen, children have cried,

And my poor streets ran red,

Warty Cromwell brought plunder and strife,

But, he also added cabbage to our diet,

Which when Raleigh's potato rotted with blight,

Helped keep rumbling, famine stricken stomachs quiet,

Jews came from Europe, were welcome and stayed,

Of their sons, two became my Lord Mayor,

War refugees, even some Vietnamese,

Culchie cousins from Kerry and Clare,

Now they're all Dubs. In Dublin.

Molly Malone, Molly Bloom,

And Parnell's mot, Kitty O'Shea,

Women of history, fable and myth,

Their memories don't fade away.

A tourist stared at our new fountain, and then,

Stopped a dealer with her pram and asked, Who is she?

That oul wan her name's Anna Livia, Sir,

Sir, she is the floozie in the jacuzzi,

South of the river, the Yuppies say,

Thank Heaven we live in Rathgar,

Howaye, is the greeting of the northerners,

Long live Charlie, eh! Are you coming for a jar?

Oh, Anna Livia how you split Dublin.

Yet, all Dubs stood together when John Paul,

Came to visit in his yellow Popemobile,

Cheering Ron Delaney and Eamonn Coughlan,

Their unity was real,

Southsider Bob Geldof made every Dubliner proud,

And when Stephen Roche rode in triumph,

All together, they clapped, long and loud,

Now the river is losing her power to divide,

For on the railway track,

The DART is whisking passengers,

From Howth to Bray, and back,

It's the travelling pride of Dublin.

Since Bang Bang rode the buses,

Shooting everyone he passed,

I've spread North and South and Westwards,

My area is now vast,

In Tallaght, Raheny, Finglas, Foxrock,

In Leinster House, and in pubs,

You will hear the voice of my people,

The special language of the Dubs.

Taxes, petrol and the pint, are expensive,

Thousands have no job,

Holes in roads keep opening, hospitals keep closing,

And now there is the problem of the smog,

In dear old dirty Dublin.

Its my Birthday, I am a thousand,

And a bit, if truth be told,

But it is a lady's privilege,

To put off growing old,

This year has been one long party,

Raheny villagers led the way,

Music, Balloons, colourful flags flying,

Right from the very first day.

An exhibition of Raheny past,

Attracted a record crowd,

There was Art, native language and culture,

And a village motto, Raheny Be Proud.

That is the real spirit of Dublin.

The ball in the Burlington was a great success,

With Gerry and Ann as Lord Mayor and Mayoress.

Maywood and Lough Derg had street parties,

Saint Annes had a barbeque,

And all the fun was reported,

In Raheny Millennium Review.

The tug of war in the village games,

Will be talked of for many a day,

The teams got longer and longer and joyously jollier,

As everyone wanted to play.

Those one thousand fine trees growing tall and straight,

Proclaim, Raheny was great in eighty-eight,

I'm a Happy Millennium Dublin.

So, children of our children's children,

Live in peace in this city, so great,

Look in our libraries, churches and annals,

To find our names, our deeds, our fate,

Some mighty buildings may crumble away,

But literature, art and music will stay,

And villages like Raheny will survive to show,

How we lived and worked, so long ago,

As a legacy, when we are gone,

We leave a task for you to do,

This city, our finest achievement, pass on,

To those coming after, from us, through you,

Then Dublin will live forever.

CELTIC TIGER – R.I.P.

It's very hard to manage here in Ireland,

The money seems to go nowhere it seems,

The poor old Celtic Tiger kicked the bucket,

The helpless cat can roar just in his dreams.

The people blamed Bertie for their troubles,

Got rid of him and his place put Brian,

It didn't solve the problem, it's got worse now,

But I suppose the poor sod's really trying.

Some brown envelopes might make a bit of difference,

But somehow I think it's far too late,

When Mary took the Med. Card from the oldies,

They marched in rage and sealed the PDs fate.

And then we found out about Mary's hairdo,

An expensive manicure that went to FAS,

And all the banks lost everybody's money,

Well not mine, I'm in the red so that's no loss.

Then Batt O'Keeffe he got a bright idea,

He'd make the classes bigger in each school,

Charge a higher registration fee for uni,

Is that Batt man a genius or a fool.

We'll all find out tomorrow when the march starts,

We might also find the car that FAS has lost,

I hope we then find who shot our tiger.

And left us bankrupt counting up the cost.

Still Christmas it is a coming, as per usual,

And Santa will bring presents never fear,

So forget your empty pockets and your worries,

Have a happy Yuletide and a bright New Year.

AT THE DENTIST

I was waiting my turn at the Dentists, and my jaw was out like that,

This guy comes and sits beside me and starts in to chat.

Said he was a farmer, with loads of sheep and cows,

Five hundred battery chickens, and two fine fat farrowing sows.

He had nearly a hundred acres, of excellent arable land,

With water running through it, and trees, a considerable stand.

I had never seen a battery chicken and I thought all trees stood up,

He took out a flask, it's poitin for my nerves said he and offered
me a sup.

He asked me was I married and I smiled and said, not yet,

What, a fine hefty hoult of a woman like you, how cheeky can you
get

I'm in the market for a wife myself, said he, a good strong one,
don't care about looks.

As long as she has decent childbearing hips and won't poison me
when she cooks.

You'd suit fine, said he, if you've a mind for the job,

Tall, healthy, strong and not too pretty,

And now that I have the electrics in and a tap in the yard,

Sure you'd never miss the city.

At that time I was an unclaimed treasure,

Meaning no man had yet fallen to my charms.

He was bald and fat and pushing sixty,

But I had heard there's money in farms.

I accepted his proposal, went with him to west Cork

And then I discovered the true meaning of hard work

I had to be up when the cock crowed to milk those loads of cows,

Chase the wandering sheep over the hills, nurse the farrowing sows

I went to see the battery chickens in their henhouse made of tin.

But though I picked them up and turned them over, I never found
where the batteries went in.

Begob, tis a fine oul cook you turned out to be,

He'd say, tucking in to dumplings in greasy stew,

Followed by apple fritters and chocolate cake with his tea,

And a drop of the creature to follow, oh yes he got that too.

Well his face grew redder and his belly grew rounder,

And one wet Tuesday he kicked the bucket,

When he was safely in the ground I put the farm on the market,

Got a great offer and swiftly took it.

So here I am back in the city where I belong,

A rich widow now, though I've found to my sorrow,

That I miss having a man around for, well I'm a full blooded woman,

So, I'm off to the dentist tomorrow.

MY SWEET BABY

He cried, did my sweet baby,

For a cuddle,

And a well loved lullaby.

His big ambition was to play,

For Manchester United,

As a forward, scoring goals.

He liked to go out fishing,

For rock salmon,

With his grandad, on the shore.

He studied hard at school,

For his examinations,

And he passed them, gaining honours.

He couldn't find a job,

For some consolation,

He chose Ecstasy, just once.

He lies under flowers as I weep,

For my sweet baby,

Who can cry no more.

DART (DUBLIN AREA RAPID TRANSIT)

Down at the station, early in the morning,

Sleep eyed commuters yawn and wait,

Talk about the weather, then compare their watches,

And assure each other that they won't be late.

A sound, a muffled rumble, a very gentle swishing,

Automatic doorways open wide,

Waiters glimpse the seats the bright green cushions,

Quickly, eagerly, they surge inside.

Closing doors perform their automatic magic,

The scenery outside goes sliding past,

No sense of motion, no chugging and no puffing,

But our early risers now are moving fast.

The City Centre terminal and everyone is hurrying,

Laggards see the time and they take heart,

So fast these trains, Dublin Area Rapid Transit,

Puffing Billy's dead, long live our DART.

AUTUMN IN ST ANNE'S

Walk with me and revel in the scent of fresh cut grass,

Listen to the wild birds lilting song,

Taste the breeze that tells of summer past and winter near,

When flowers fade and evening time grows long.

Walk with me and see the leaves just fallen, red and gold,

They make lovely carpet as they die,

Newly naked branches, liberated, reaching up,

To sketch intricate lace against the sky.

Walk with me and meet and greet our neighbours and our friends,

Join in all our next year's social plans,

Be a happy part of this community we share,

Walk with me in Autumn in Saint Anne's.

ROSA

Our road became quiet when the children grew up,

The boys and girls who ran and played,

Most are married now, some are abroad,

Only a very few have stayed.

Lonely people looked out of the windows,

Seeing in memory the laughter filled street,

Wishing to hear the shouts that once echoed,

Straining for the patter of tiny feet,

Suddenly into the void came a chuckle,

A flash of red coat and a gleam of blonde hair,

New neighbours moved in and our spirits were lifted,

Rose had come our lives to share.

Six years old and a bundle of mischief,

Lively, noisy, inquisitive, bright,

With baby twin brothers who soon will join her,

Filling our empty street with delight.

Again, after years, there'll be balls in the garden,

Youth and vigour will once again reign,

Hopefully the first of many new children,

Rosa enlivens our road again.

DOROTHY

She died last week, and all alone,

I didn't know she ailed,

Though I had noticed how slowly she walked,

And that her ruddy cheeks had paled.

I only met Dorothy in old age,

With family grown and scattered,

Never saw her husband, the love of her life,

Wasn't there when her children's feet pattered.

She took her little white dog for walks,

And chatted to neighbours she met,

Went to ten o'clock Mass every morning,

Even on days that were wet.

I never heard her moan or complain,

Or criticise what others might do,

She always said she was feeling fine,

And then would ask, "how are you?"

I didn't know the baby she was,

The young girl, the mother, the wife,

But the wonderful lady I met in old age,

Has greatly enriched my life.

I will miss Dorothy now she is gone,

But now I have a friend up above,

I will remember her smile, her good advice,

A gentle old lady, full of love.

MONDAY MORNING

Stop the alarm, crawl up in the dark,

Stub a toe, on the leg of the bed,

One shoe missing, who came up here and moved it?

Oh! This aching, splitting head.

Fill the kettle, turn the gas on,

Where's the matches, search high and low,

This water is taking so long to boil,

What's the time, half eight, oh! No.

No time now for egg and rasher,

Make do with weak tea and a crust,

The car! It won't start! Frost has gripped it,

Means I'll have to take the bus.

Standing at the bus stop waiting,

That nosy chap next door, called Jim,

Last time we met he paid my bus fare,

Suppose now I must pay for him.

Twenty past nine, sneak into the office,

Bump straight into the boss, is my face red,

Late again, what's your story this time?

The junior giggles, wish I was dead.

Struggle through the work, at last it's nearly lunchtime,

Now, slam shut the book, fling down the pen,

Whistle a gay tune, life is worth living,

Till Monday morning comes again.

MY WEEK

Everything went wrong for me on Monday,

I got up late, and found the budgie bald,

The vet said, stimulate him, cheer him up,

He's plucked his plumage out because he bored.

I wondered how I could give him some amusement,

Make his feathers grow back by gladdening his little soul,

Then I got it! I moved his cage over to the sideboard,

Where we could watch the goldfish, swimming round their bowl.

He was more than amused, he tried to get out and go fishing,

The two goldfish weren't much impressed by that,

They swam faster and faster in terror, jumped out of the water,

And were promptly pounced on and swallowed by the cat.

Tuesday I was set on by our neighbour,

She complained about the dandelions in my garden,

Nasty things, they're weeds, she roared, quite fiercely,

Off with their heads, they don't deserve a pardon.

I argued that they were a thing of beauty,

Displaying their golden petals to the sun,

And blowing the ginnyjoes to see if a lover is faithful,

Gives the children hours of harmless fun.

It was no good. Wednesday found me weeding, as she watched me,

To those lovely flowers I dealt out death,

But I suffered for it, the grass gave me hay fever,

And all day Thursday I couldn't catch my breath.

Out shopping on Friday, I took a gander at the fountain,

The new one in O'Connell Street,

Do you know what's on it, an oul wan called Anna Livia,

Nearly stark naked from her head down to her feet.

And she lying there, in this great big pool of water,

A brazen hussy, in the middle of our city,

At least Nelson, on his column, kept his clothes on,

And if you climbed up the steps, the view was really pretty.

I enjoyed myself at the swimming pool on Saturday,

I could do the breast stroke if I could only let go of the bar,

Yer woman next door, that doesn't like dandelions, like a mermaid,
she could swim the Channel,

I hate people like that, still there you are.

Sunday was my birthday, the other half gave me a card,

And a box of sweets, it was nice of him, pity the sweets were hard

And I couldn't eat them, not with my teeth, anyway sweets make
you fat,

And when a girl gets to my age, you know yourself, you have to be
careful of things like that.

It's not that I'm feeling old, but, I'm over twenty-one,

And if life begins at forty, Well, mine is well begun.

Next week might be better, I might win the lottery, A quarter of a
million, just think of that,

I'd buy a little fluffy jacket for my bald budgie, Two new goldfish,
and a muzzle for the cat.

TO A MOTORIST

Sitting there as you powerful beast,

Snorts and fumes at the traffic lights,

Unconscious finger exploring your nose,

Eyes on a long legged girl in tights,

One hand on the wheel, keeping the beat,

As your radio spills noise on to the street,

Do you think of all the people who pass,

Rushing along on their way to Mass.

Do you see them as children, Mums and Dads,

With hopes and dreams, foibles and fads,

Or as obstacles that bar your way,

As on to the road in front they stray,

When the lights change and you drive again,

Do you remember those women and men,

Do you realise how privileged you are,

To be able to drive your motor car?

DOWNTOWN DECEMBER

Spring can be beautiful, as can Summer, and Autumn,

But the season I like to remember,

Is that magical time that comes once a year,

In Dublin, downtown, in December.

As carol singers chorus, traders call,

Get your long decorating chains,

The last of the jumping jacks,

Ten pence each the starlights,

Mechanical trains on tracks.

Away in a manger, no crib for a bed…

Do you want some glittering tinsel, Ma'am?

Or a star for your Christmas tree,

And look at these lovely fairy lights,

You get two spare bulbs for free.

The first Noel the angels did sing...

Hey, Mister, buy a balloon for the child,

A nice red one, or maybe a blue,

Them long ones, they're only 30p Sir,

Ah! Sure! Give us 50p for the two.

Once in Royal David's city, stood a lonely cattle shed...

Only one left now, the bucking bronco,

Roll up folks and see him go,

Get the last of your cuddly toys,

Donald Duck, and Pinnochio.

Silent night, Holy night...

CHRISTMAS RUSH

I met a woman in Henry Street on the 15th of September,

She was buying the sort of things I buy,

On the twenty fourth of December,

Gloves for Grandad, socks for Jim,

A record gift token for Maurice,

For green fingered Luke, a gardening book,

And pretty earrings for Dorie.

I like to be finished the presents, said she,

Before October is here,

For with all the Christmas cooking,

It's the busiest time of the year.

I make loads of plum puddings mixed with stout,

And a little rum, to taste,

Rich fruit cakes, I make, ready to top,

With Royal Icing and almond paste.

She was all organised, no last minute rush,

Christmas wouldn't take her by surprise,

No frantic searching for fairy light bulbs,

Or slippers, in Uncle Tom's size.

No panic buying, no sudden fear,

That everything won't get done,

I wondered, would she ever realise,

She was missing all the fun.

STORM EMMA

The snow fell down and down and down,
Covered fields and roads, city and town,
Sheep on the hillsides, the cattle on grass,
Motorised traffic stopped, nothing could pass.

Code red, code red, nobody should go out,
Television, radio, and newspapers did shout.
Then, to add to the bitter cold and snow,
Ferocious wind from the east began to blow.

Snowploughs battled the awful conditions,
Day and night they continued their missions,
No schools were open, the children were glad,
No work meant no money, so parents were sad.

Four days of misery, a slow thaw came at last,
But March tides were rising, rivers filling up fast.
Flooding threatened, sandbags were laid out,
Storm Emma is passing, the Media did shout.

The rain poured down and down, and down,

On each field and village, city and town.

Traffic was flowing, we welcomed the rain,

Ireland was returning to normal again.

Then our capricious climate produced a trick,

Despite torrential rain, floods, and snow so thick,

It seems Storm Emma had a beastly daughter,

For we got a countrywide shortage, of water.

DADDY'S LITTLE HELPER

What are you trying to do Daddy,

What are you trying to make,

Mam said if I come out to help you,

She will cook a chocolate cake.

Do you want to see my pet caterpillar,

I keep him in this matchbox, look Dad, see,

I feed him lettuce leaves and bits of cabbage,

Some day he will grow up as big as me.

Myra says he will grow to be a dragon,

Could he really, Dad, would he eat me up,

Or is Myra only being jealous, Dad,

Because her pet is just a little pup.

Why has the shoe last got three feet Dad,

Do you know who puts the lines on a screw,

You know, you never answered my question,

Dad, what are you trying to do?

In school this morning, Teacher asked me

What is nine multiplied by four,

I thought I knew, but got the answer wrong,

And Teacher made me stand outside the door.

Then Sister Mary Celestine came along,

And sent me for an errand to the corner shop,

Six red and blue lined copies and an eraser,

And told me I could buy a lollipop.

Be careful, that hammer is very heavy Daddy,

When you bang it down it sounds like a drum

Ah, Daddy, did it hit you, ah, poor Daddy,

Look, I can see blood on your thumb.

Mam says you are a lucky man, Daddy,

To have a great helping hand like me, but,

You never said what you are trying to make,

Daddy, when it is finished, what will it be?

THE RUNNING QUESTION

What do you do all day, I'd say

Here in this house while I'm away,

Surely it can't take you all day, I'd say

To make a bed and prepare a meal.

Why don't you do something, I'd say

Like go into town; take in a play.

Just what do you do all day

While I'm away?

Nothing at all she would say

Just smile as if to say

You will see what you have to say

Some day when your daughter asks

What do you do all day?

What do you do all day, my daughters say

While I'm away.

It can't take you all day

To make a bed, prepare a meal.

What do you do all day?

It can't take all that long

To keep the house spick and clean.

What do you do all day while we're away?

My daughters say.

I know what I'D like to say.

There's dishes to clean, potatoes to peel,

Beds to make, meals to bake,

The washing to watch as it hangs on the line,

Hoping to rescue it from the rain in time.

The shopping to do; their books to renew.

The ironing to sort, fuel to be bought.

That's what I'd like to say.

Instead a silent prayer wends its way

To the one who listened in silence

When I'd say

Just what do you do all day while I'M away?

OUT THERE

What is out there, among the stars,

Above the Earth, Moon, Sun and even Mars,

Do others sit and gaze out as I do,

Thinking, dreaming, wondering what or who

Might occupy a place they cannot see,

Far away and bathed in mystery.

Sometime, somehow, when dreams come true,

We will be face to face, us and you,

Shall we meet each other as friend or foe,

Or just joyfully embrace and say hello,

My hope is that the latter is true.

And that together we can search the view,

Discovering the truth of what else is there,

And making new friends everywhere.

DISCOVERY

The house is tidy, sweet-smelling, big,

The last of my children has married and gone,

I am alone.

Even the cat has gone travelling off,

Football scarred grass in the garden has grown,

I am alone.

There is no gear to be washed for the match,

Homework is finished, lessons all learned,

I am alone.

Nearly thirty years of mothering finished,

Nobody needs me, I am alone, and at last,

Free.

JUNE COOKE

June is a Dubliner who has lived most of her life in Raheny. Mother of four sons and three daughters, with twenty-three grandchildren, her life is a busy one.

Apart from writing, June likes to paint pictures, grow flowers, and play keyboard music. Active in several organizations such as Girl Guiding, Ladies Clubs, and Toastmasters, she likes to read or play computer games in any free time she can grab.

Printed in Great Britain
by Amazon